Play
rresents
Louisa May Alcott's

Little Women
FOR KIDS
(The melodramatic version!)

For 6-16 actors, or kids of all ages who want to have fun!
Creatively modified by Khara C. Barnhart and Brendan P. Kelso
Cover illustrated by Shana Hallmeyer
Cover Character illustrated by Ron Leishman
Louisa May Alcott character created by Ryan Gottleib

3 Melodramatic Modifications of Alcott's play
for 3 different group sizes:

6-8 actors

9-12 actors

13-16 actors

Table Of Contents

Foreword .... Pg 4

School, Afterschool, and Summer classes .... Pg 6

Performance Rights .... Pg 6

6-8 Actors .... Pg 8

9-12 Actors .... Pg 32

13-16 Actors .... Pg 60

Special Thanks .... Pg 89

Sneak Peeks at other Playing With Plays .... Pg 90

About the Authors .... Pg 104

For my mom,
who gave me my first copy of Little Women
when I was seven years old.

-KCB

To the little women in my life,
may you always be strong, kind, and amazing!

-Dad

Playing with Plays™ – Louisa May Alcott's Little Women for Kids

Copyright © 2004-2020 by Brendan P. Kelso, Playing with Plays
Some characters on the cover are ©Ron Leishman ToonClipart.com

All rights reserved. No part of this book may be reproduced in any form or by any electronic or mechanical means, including photocopying, recording, information storage or retrieval systems now known or to be invented, without permission in writing from the publisher, except by a reviewer, who may quote brief passages in a review, written for inclusion within a periodical. Any members of education institutions wishing to photocopy part or all of the work for classroom use, or publishers who would like to obtain permission to include the work in an anthology, should send their inquiries to the publisher. We monitor the internet for cases of piracy and copyright infringement/violations. We will pursue all cases within the full extent of the law.

Whenever a Playing With Plays play is produced, the following must be included on all programs, printing and advertising for the play: © Brendan P. Kelso, Playing with Plays, www.PlayingWithPlays.com. All rights reserved.

CAUTION: Professionals and amateurs are hereby warned that these plays are subject to a royalty. They are fully protected, in whole, in part, or in any form under the copyright laws of the United States, Canada, the British Empire, and all other countries of the Copyright Union, and are subject to royalty. All rights, including professional, amateur, motion picture, radio, television, recitation, public reading, internet, and any method of photographic reproduction are strictly reserved.

For performance rights please see page 6 of this book or contact:

contact@PlayingWithPlays.com

-Please note, for certain circumstances, we do waive copyright and performance fees.
Rules subject to change

www.PlayingWithPlays.com

Printed in the United States of America

ISBN: 9781705948002

Foreword

When I was in high school there was something about Shakespeare that appealed to me. Not that I understood it mind you, but there were clear scenes and images that always stood out in my mind. Romeo & Juliet, "Romeo, Romeo; wherefore art thou Romeo?"; Julius Caesar, "Et tu Brute"; Macbeth, "Double, Double, toil and trouble"; Hamlet, "to be or not to be"; A Midsummer Night's Dream, all I remember about this was a wickedly cool fairy and something about a guy turning into a donkey that I thought was pretty funny. It was not until I started analyzing Shakespeare's plays as an actor that I realized one very important thing, I still didn't understand them. Seriously though, it's tough enough for adults, let alone kids. Then it hit me, why don't I make a version that kids could perform, but make it easy for them to understand with a splash of Shakespeare lingo mixed in? And voila! A melodramatic masterpiece was created! They are intended to be melodramatically fun!

THE PLAYS: There are 3 plays within this book, for three different group sizes. The reason: to allow educators or parents to get the story across to their children regardless of the size of their group. As you read through the plays, there are several lines that are highlighted. These are actual lines from the original book. I am a little more particular about the kids saying these lines verbatim. But the rest, well... have fun!

The entire purpose of this book is to instill the love of a classic story, as well as drama, into the kids.

And when you have children who have a passion for something, they will start to teach themselves, with or without school.

These plays are intended for pure fun. Please DO NOT have the kids learn these lines verbatim, that would be a complete waste of creativity. But do have them basically know their lines and improvise wherever they want as long as it pertains to telling the story. Because that is the goal of an actor: to tell the story. In A Midsummer Night's Dream, I once had a student playing Quince question me about one of her lines, "but in the actual story, didn't the Mechanicals state that 'they would hang us'?" I thought for a second and realized that she had read the story with her mom, and she was right. So I let her add the line she wanted and it added that much more fun, it made the play theirs. I have had kids throw water on the audience, run around the audience, sit in the audience, lose their pumpkin pants (size 30 around a size 15 doesn't work very well, but makes for some great humor!) and most importantly, die all over the stage. The kids love it.

One last note: if you want some educational resources, loved our plays, want to tell the world how much your kids loved performing Shakespeare, want to insult someone with our Shakespeare Insult Generator, or are just a fan of Shakespeare, then hop on our website and have fun:

PlayingWithPlays.com

With these notes, I'll see you on the stage, have fun, and break a leg!

SCHOOL, AFTERSCHOOL, and SUMMER classes

I've been teaching these plays as afterschool and summer programs for quite some time. Many people have asked what the program is, therefore, I have put together a basic formula so any teacher or parent can follow and have melodramatic success! As well, many teachers use my books in a variety of ways. You can view the formula and many more resources on my website at: PlayingWithPlays.com

- Brendan

OTHER PLAYS AND FULL LENGTH SCRIPTS

We have over 25 different titles, as well as a full-length play in 4-acts for theatre groups: Shakespeare's Hilarious Tragedies. You can see all of our other titles on our website here: PlayingWithPlays.com/books

As well, you can see a sneak peek at some of those titles at the back of this book.

And, if you ever have any questions, please don't hesitate to ask at: Contact@PlayingWithPlays.com

ROYALTIES

If you have any questions about royalties or performance licenses, here are the basic guidelines:

1) Please contact us! We always LOVE to hear about a school or group performing our books! We would also love to share photos and brag about your program as well! (with your permission, of course)

2) If you are a group and DO NOT charge your kids to be in this production, contact us about discounted copyright fees (one way or another, we will make this work for you!) You are NOT required to buy a book per kid (but, we will still send you some really cool Shakespeare tattoos for your kids!)

3) If you are a group and DO charge your kids to be in the production, (i.e. afterschool program, summer camp) we ask that you purchase a book per kid. Contact us as we will give you a bulk discount (10 books or more) and send some really cool press on Shakespeare tattoos!

4) If you are a group and DO NOT charge the audience to see the plays, please see our website FAQs to see if you are eligible to waive the performance royalties (most performances are eligible).

5) If you are a group and DO charge the audience to see the performance, please see our website FAQs for performance licensing fees (this includes performances for donations and competitions).

Any other questions or comments, please see our website or email us at:

contact@PlayingWithPlays.com

The 15-Minute or so Little Women for Kids

by Louisa May Alcott
Creatively modified by Khara C. Barnhart
and Brendan P. Kelso

6-8 Actors

CAST OF CHARACTERS:

JOSEPHINE MARCH (JO): aspiring writer and sarcastically snarky

MARGARET MARCH (MEG): the oldest March sister

BETH MARCH: another March sister, quiet and sweet, ALWAYS nice

AMY MARCH: the youngest March sister

[1]**MARMEE:** the March sisters' mom

[1]**AUNT MARCH:** grumpy aunt of the March sisters

THE REST...

[2]**THEODORE LAURENCE (LAURIE):** the boy next door, likes Jo, but marries Amy

[2]**FRIEDRICH BHAER:** kind professor and (later) Jo's husband

The same actors can play the following parts:
[1]MARMEE and AUNT MARCH
[2]BHAER and LAURIE
(HOWEVER, Bhaer's line in the last scene will need to be deleted, AND one character should wear a hat or mustache, since both characters like Jo and we don't want to confuse the audience!)

ACT 1 SCENE 1

(enter JO, MEG, BETH, and AMY)

JO: Christmas won't be Christmas without any presents!

MEG: It's so dreadful to be poor!

AMY: I don't think it's fair for some girls to have plenty of things, and other girls nothing at all.

BETH: *(happily)* We've got Father, Mother, and each other! What else could we POSSIBLY want! *(JO, MEG, and AMY all roll their eyes and sigh)*

JO: *(to audience, pointing at sisters)* That's Beth. She's the good sister. That's Meg, the oldest, and that's Amy, the youngest, and I'm Jo. So now you're all caught up.

(enter MARMEE)

MARCH SISTERS: Marmee!

JO: *(to audience)* Anybody can be called "mom." Only superstar moms are called "Marmee."

MARMEE: Girls! I have a letter from your father who has been away at war! *(reads letter)* Give them all of my dear love and a kiss. Remind them to be good so that when I come back to them I may be fonder and prouder than ever of my little women.

BETH: Of course we will, Marmee!

MARMEE: Speaking of being good, I know it's Christmas and we're poor, but there's a much poorer family down the street and I think we should give them our breakfast!

(pause; they all look at each other)

MARCH SISTERS: Um, sure…

MARMEE: Great! Let's pack up our delicious Christmas breakfast. Hooray!

MARCH SISTERS: *(not very excited)* Yeah… hooray.

(ALL exit)

ACT 1 SCENE 2

(enter JO and MEG)

MEG: Please be cool at this party, Jo. Hold your shoulder straight, and take short steps, and don't shake hands if you are introduced to anyone. It isn't the thing.

JO: Fine! So, which shoulder should I hold straight, left or right?

MEG: *(glares at JO)* And DON'T BE RUDE!

JO: I feel so awkward at events like this!

MEG: I'm going to dance with my friends. Be good, Jo.

(MEG runs to the corner of the stage and begins dancing; enter LAURIE, walking slowly backward, looking overwhelmed; he bumps into JO)

JO: Oh!

LAURIE: Sorry! Wait! You live near my grandpa and me, don't you?

JO: Um, yeah. Next door. You're Mr. Laurence, right? I'm Jo.

LAURIE: I'm not Mr. Laurence, I'm only Laurie.

JO: Laurie Laurence, what an odd name. *(pause)* Whoops! That was rude, wasn't it?

MEG: *(calls from across the stage)* Yep! That was rude!

JO: *(under breath)* Fiddlesticks! *(to Laurie)* Why do you live with your grandpa?

LAURIE: My parents are dead.

JO: Bummer. Want to be best friends forever and ever?

LAURIE: Yes, I do!

JO: Fantastic!

(ALL exit)

ACT 1 SCENE 3

(enter JO, MEG, and AMY; there are a bunch of papers on the floor)

AMY: Girls, where are you going?

JO: Never mind. Little girls shouldn't ask questions.

AMY: WHAT?!

MEG: We're going to see a play with Laurie.

JO: And you can't come, 'cause you're a little girl!

AMY: Am not!

JO: Too bad, so sad! Farewell, baby Amy! *(JO and MEG exit quickly)*

AMY: *(calls after them)* You'll be sorry for this, Jo March, see if you ain't! What's this? *(she picks up the bunch of papers dramatically and exits as MEG and JO reenter)*

MEG: Wow, what a great play!

JO: Yep! Wait! *(looks around)* Where is my book? The one I JUST wrote? You know, the papers that were right here? *(points to floor)*

(enter AMY looking suspicious)

JO: Amy, you've got it!

AMY: You'll never see your silly old book again! I burned it up! "Little girls" can play with fire, you know. Muahahahahaha!

JO: *(screams)* Nooooooooooooooooooooooooooo! That was the only copy in the world! It was my masterpiece! I'll never forgive you as long as I live.

(enter MARMEE)

MARMEE: *(to JO)* My dear, don't let the sun go down upon your anger. Forgive each other, and begin again tomorrow.

JO: She doesn't deserve to be forgiven. Do you even realize how hard it is living up to your expectations, Marmee? Man! Parents' expectations can be brutal! I'm outta here. I'm going ice-skating with Laurie. He gets me.

(JO begins walking across the stage with AMY sneaking behind her; MARMEE and MEG exit; LAURIE enters and links arms with JO; they begin "skating" around the stage, laughing)

LAURIE: *(to JO)* Stay away from the middle; the ice is thin!

(JO notices AMY "skating" across the stage)

JO: *(to audience)* If I weren't so mad at her, I'd warn her about the thin ice. But she's the one who wanted to play with fire! *(mimicking AMY's evil laugh)* Muahahahaha indeed!

(AMY falls dramatically to the floor)

AMY: Help! I fell through the ice! I'm drowning! And freezing! It's so cooooooold!

(JO and LAURIE rush over and pull AMY up; AMY coughs and shudders)

JO: This is all my fault! It's my dreadful temper! I could have warned her, and I didn't!

(enter MARMEE)

MARMEE: Don't worry. Amy will be fine.

AMY: *(gives a really shaky thumb's up)* Tot-tal-YYYYYYY.

MARMEE: *(to JO)* But that temper of yours needs to be controlled.

JO: I will try, Mother, I truly will. But you must help me, remind me, and keep me from flying out!

MARMEE: No problem! That's what mothers are for!

(ALL exit)

ACT 1 SCENE 4

(enter LAURIE, JO, MEG, BETH, and AMY)

LAURIE: What a beautiful day for a picnic! Welcome to Camp Laurence!

AMY: So, what should we do?

JO: We could put on a play!

MEG: Uh, Jo... we're IN a play. *(motions to audience)* And we don't need to do the "play within a play" thing. This isn't Shakespeare.

JO: Fine.

MEG: Truth or dare?

BETH: Oh, we couldn't! It wouldn't be proper!

AMY: You're so boring, Beth. This is the worst picnic ever.

LAURIE: *(whispers loudly to JO)* Hey, guess what? You know my tutor, John? Well, he totally has a crush on Meg!

JO: How do you know?

LAURIE: He's been keeping one of her gloves in his pocket! I catch him looking at it ALL the time. Isn't that romantic?

JO: No, it's horrid! What is he, some kind of stalker? I wish you hadn't told me! I don't want anybody to take Meg away from me. Ugh, this day is ruined; have fun at your picnic without me! *(JO exits and everyone else shrugs and follows her offstage)*

MEG: Told you we should have played Truth or Dare!

ACT 1 SCENE 5

(enter JO, MEG, BETH, AMY, and LAURIE; entire scene is to audience)

LAURIE: And now, to lighten the mood…

ALL: Presenting: Our castles in the air!

LAURIE: Otherwise known as our hopes and dreams for the future.

MEG: I should like a lovely house… and heaps of money!

AMY: I want to be the best artist in the whole world! *(holds up stick figure drawing)*

JO: And I want to do something heroic or wonderful that won't be forgotten after I'm dead. I think I shall write books, and get rich and famous.

LAURIE: I want to be a famous musician! *(strums a few painful chords on a guitar)*

(ALL CHARACTERS turn and look at BETH)

BETH: I want to stay at home safe with Father and Mother, and help take care of the family.

JO: And that's why she's the good one.

LAURIE: Only the good die young, Beth.

JO: *(to LAURIE, while pointing at audience)* Shhhhh! No spoilers! Don't ruin it for them!

LAURIE: *(to audience)* Sorry. *(whispers)* Not sorry.

(JO pushes LAURIE offstage grumbling under her breath; ALL exit)

ACT 1 SCENE 6

(enter JO, MEG, BETH, and AMY)

MEG: While Marmee's out of town, we are supposed to go help that poor family again, remember?

BETH: I'll do it! I love helping people! *(BETH exits)*

JO: So, I was thinking about a new story I could write about...

(enter BETH, stumbling around)

BETH: The poor family has scarlet fever! Their baby died! And now I have scarlet fever! *(she falls dramatically to the ground)*

AMY: Oh no! This is awful!

MEG: *(feels BETH'S forehead)* I don't think she's going to make it!

JO: No! We are only halfway through the play, she can't die... yet!

MEG: I wish I had no heart, it aches so!

AMY: *(pushes MEG out of the way feels BETH'S forehead)* Wait! She's definitely going to live... for now!

MEG & JO: Hooray!

BETH: I'm better now, but I have the strangest feeling that I'll never be quite as healthy as I was before...

AMY: This is no time for doom and gloom! Let's go celebrate!

(ALL exit)

ACT 1 SCENE 7

(enter MEG)

MEG: *(to audience)* I have a secret! I'm so in love with John the tutor! I know I'm too young to get married, but I totally want to!

(enter AUNT MARCH carrying a giant bag of money)

AUNT MARCH: There's mischief going on, and I insist upon knowing what it is! Wait! You're not going to marry that John person are you, Meg?

MEG: Aunt March! What are you doing here? Are you psychic? How is this even your business?

AUNT MARCH: You cannot marry that lowly tutor. If you do, not one penny of my money ever goes to you!

MEG: Excuse me? I shall marry whom I please, Aunt March, and you can leave your money to anyone you like.

AUNT MARCH: Then I'm done with you forever! Goodbye! *(AUNT MARCH exits)*

MEG: I'll show her! First, we need to speed things up. *(calls offstage)* Uh, Jo! A little help?

(JO runs onstage holding a sign that says THREE YEARS LATER, hands it to MEG, and runs back offstage)

MEG: Perfect! Well, now that I'm old enough, I'm going to go get hitched! *(calls offstage)* John, my love! Let's get married! I'll need my glove back...

(MEG exits)

ACT 2 SCENE 1

(enter JO, MEG, BETH, AMY, and MARMEE)

JO: Guess what everybody? I wrote a silly, romance-adventure story and it's going to be published, and they gave me a hundred dollars! That's like 3,000 dollars today!

BETH: That's amazing!

MEG: Good job, Jo!

MARMEE: A sensationalist story? Hmm. You can do better than this Jo. Aim at the highest, and never mind the money.

AMY: I think the money is the best part of it.

JO: You're right, Amy! Now I can send Beth and Mother to the seaside so Beth can feel better and not die like we keep alluding to. See how generous I am? Now, I'm going to write a novel!

MARMEE: Don't put too much description in it!

MEG: Don't forget to add some tragedy!

AMY: And don't make it too fun!

JO: Right. Thanks for the advice, everyone!

BETH: I should like to see it printed soon!

JO: Me too, Beth, me too!

BETH: Preferably by page 28, because, well… you know… *(makes a "dead" looking face)*

JO: Page 28, got it!

(ALL exit)

ACT 2 SCENE 2

(enter JO, AMY, AUNT MARCH; AUNT MARCH holds giant bag of money)

AUNT MARCH: So tell me, girls, who is the nicer sister?

(AMY and JO look at each other)

AMY: I am.

JO: She is.

AUNT MARCH: Hmm, okay. And do either of you speak French?

AMY: Oui! Oo la la!

JO: Don't know a word. I'm very stupid about studying anything, can't bear French, it's such a slippery, silly sort of language.

AUNT MARCH: Well then, since Jo hates French, Amy gets to travel to Europe with Aunt Carrol as her young companion. Want to go, Amy?

AMY: Is that even a question? YES! Or should I say, bien sûr! Wait. Who's Aunt Carrol?

AUNT MARCH: She's your other aunt. Her name is Carrol. It's really not difficult to figure out.

JO: Oh my tongue! My abominable tongue! Why can't I keep my big mouth shut!

AUNT MARCH: Maybe someday you'll learn, dear. But, I doubt it. Bye, Bye!

(ALL exit)

ACT 2 SCENE 3

(enter JO and LAURIE)

JO: So, Laurie, how many girls have you sent flowers to this week?

LAURIE: Nobody. Yet...

JO: Mother doesn't approve of flirting even in fun, and you do flirt desperately, Laurie.

LAURIE: Because it's fun! Jo, you should try it sometime.

JO: I really don't know how.

LAURIE: Take lessons of Amy, she has a regular talent for it.

JO: Laurie, all this flirting talk is making me really uncomfortable. *(to audience)* I think he's beginning to "LIKE me" like me. Instead of just like me. *(to LAURIE)* Look, I have no time to learn how to flirt since I'll be moving to New York right away.

LAURIE: It won't do a bit of good, Jo. My eye is on you, so mind what you do, or I'll come and bring you home.

JO: You'll do no such thing. Look, the big city is calling me, so good luck and goodbye!

(JO and LAURIE exit in different directions)

ACT 2 SCENE 4

(enter JO)

JO: *(to audience)* Here I am living in New York, just like a real writer! I live in a boarding house with some sweet families and this super cool German professor, Friedrich Bhaer… *(enter BHAER)*

BHAER: *(with German accent)* Hallo, Jo. So, you peep at me, I peep at you, and this is not bad, but see, I am not pleasanting when I say, haf you a wish for German?

JO: Excuse me?

BHAER: Would you like me to teach you German? Please say ja. That's yes. First lesson! *(offers JO a high five; JO ignores him)*

JO: Sure, why not? But this isn't, like, a date, right? Because you have to be at least forty. That's really old.

BHAER: Ha! Well, let's just say I'm young at heart. Come on; we have a lot of work to do!

(JO and BHAER exit)

ACT 2 SCENE 5

(enter JO)

JO: *(to audience)* And just like that, the year is over and I'm back home! New York was fun, and I'll miss my good friend, Professor Bhaer, but my family needs me here.

(enter LAURIE)

LAURIE: Jo! Thank goodness you're home. I've missed you so much this past year! I have something super important to ask you...

JO: No, Laurie. Please don't!

LAURIE: You don't even know what I'm going to say! Look, Jo. I've loved you ever since I've known you. Will you marry me, pretty please?

JO: See, I knew what you were going to say. *(to audience)* Boys are so predictable.

LAURIE: Well?

JO: Nein.

LAURIE: Nine?

JO: No... NEIN. It's German for NO. You're my best friend. It would be so weird!

LAURIE: Hold on. You love that old man, don't you? The *(air quotes)* "professor?"

JO: No, I don't! *(to audience)* Wait... do I? Oh man, I might.

LAURIE: I'm so sad! *(starts melodramatically crying)*

JO: You should probably take a trip somewhere. Travel is good for the heart!

LAURIE: Nothing can fix my broken, mutilated, utterly destroyed heart! But Europe does sound cool. Thanks, Jo. And goodbye!

(ALL exit)

ACT 2 SCENE 6

(enter JO and BETH)

JO: You look terrible, Beth.

BETH: I never really got over that bout of scarlet fever. I think I need another trip to the seashore.

JO: Let's do it! *(they link arms and skip around stage)* Ahhhhhhhhhhh, the ocean air! So fresh! And *(sniffs the air)*... fishy. And sort of stinky, but...

BETH: Listen, Jo, I looked ahead in the play, and I'm going to die soon.

JO: What? NO! Beth, you must get well!

BETH: I want to! But, you know, I can't change the plot!

JO: Well, the plot is dumb.

BETH: Can't argue with you there. Let's just enjoy the time we have left, shall we?

JO: You're too good for this world, Beth.

BETH: I know, Jo. I know.

(ALL exit)

ACT 2 SCENE 7

(enter AMY and LAURIE from opposite sides of the stage)

AMY: Laurie?!

LAURIE: Amy! Bonjour! Fancy meeting you over here in France.

AMY: *(to audience)* He's looking good!

LAURIE: *(to audience)* Wow! She's all grown up! And so pretty!

(they look at each other and giggle)

LAURIE: How about we row this boat around the lake?

AMY: Let's do it!

(they sit side-by-side onstage and mime rowing a boat, perfectly in sync)

AMY: How well we pull together, don't we?

LAURIE: So well that I wish we might always pull in the same boat. Get it?

AMY: Are you saying we should get married?

LAURIE: Yep!

AMY: *(to audience)* Yes, I know he proposed to my sister first. Don't judge. He's dreamy! *(to LAURIE)* I'm in! *(they high five and exit)*

ACT 2 SCENE 8

(enter JO, MEG, MARMEE, and BETH; BETH lies down onstage and everyone else gathers around her)

BETH: Well everyone, it's time for me to go.

(ALL CHARACTERS are crying or sniffling)

MEG: This is terrible!

MARMEE: My baby!

BETH: I love you all! And remember... love is the only thing we can carry with us when we go, and it makes the end so easy!

(BETH dies melodramatically; ALL characters wail and cry; Beth gets up and twirls herself offstage while the rest of the characters wave to her and blow her kisses)

MEG: She'll always be our angel!!

JO: *(to audience)* Louisa May Alcott. Making readers cry since 1868.

(ALL exit)

ACT 2 SCENE 9

(enter JO)

JO: *(to audience)* An old maid, that's what I'm to be. A literary spinster, with a pen for a spouse! I mean, I'm almost twenty-five! Ugh!

(enter BHAER)

BHAER: Hallo, Jo!

JO: What are you doing here?

BHAER: Oh, you know, I was just… conveniently passing through your town…

JO: Well, I'm always glad to see you, sir.

BHAER: I got a new job, and I'm moving to the West.

JO: Congratulations, but unfortunately, you can't go… because I love you!

BHAER: Now I will haf to show thee all my heart, and I so gladly will, because thou must take care of it hereafter! That means I love you, too!

JO: You're SO romantic! I don't even care that you're old!

BHAER: Just like stinky cheese, I get better with age!

(JO and BHAER stay on stage)

ACT 2 SCENE 10

(AUNT MARCH enters)

AUNT MARCH: I'm very old and it's time for me to die. But I wanted to let you know I'm leaving you my house! *(she hands JO a set of keys and then dies)*

JO: Aunt March! *(looks down at AUNT MARCH on the floor)* Um, thank you? *(steps over body, to BHAER)* I know what we can do with that big old house! I want to open a school for little lads—a good, happy, homelike school! And you can teach them!

BHAER: That I can do!

(ALL exit)

ACT 2 SCENE 11

(enter JO, BHAER, MEG, AMY, LAURIE, and MARMEE)

MARMEE: Oh, my girls, however long you may live, I never can wish you a greater happiness than this!

MEG: *(to audience)* By "this," Marmee means domestic life.

AMY: Right! We all end up with husbands, houses, and children. Oh, and laundry. So much laundry.

JO: But where's the intrigue! The scandal! The adventure!

LAURIE: *(interrupting)* Oh, come on, Jo. You've gotta know your audience. People like happy endings.

JO: *(to audience)* Well. I'd love to offer you a more exciting ending than "they all lived happily ever after," but hey, that's all she wrote. Literally. Until the sequel anyway...

LAURIE: Wait. There's a sequel?

BETH: *(pops her head onstage)* It's called Little Men. *(whispers dramatically)* Not as popular.

BHAER: Looks like we have some work to do, Laurie!

MEG: And on that note...

ALL: *(with bravado)* THE END!

(ALL CHARACTERS wave goodbye to the audience and exit)

The 20-Minute or so Little Women for Kids
by Louisa May Alcott
Creatively modified by Khara C. Barnhart
and Brendan P. Kelso
9-12 Actors

CAST OF CHARACTERS:
JOSEPHINE MARCH (JO): aspiring writer and sarcastically snarky
MARGARET MARCH (MEG): the oldest March sister
BETH MARCH: another March sister, quiet and sweet, ALWAYS nice
AMY MARCH: the youngest March sister
[1]**MARMEE:** the March sisters' mom
[2]**MR. MARCH:** the March sisters' dad
AUNT MARCH: grumpy aunt of the March sisters
THE REST...
THEODORE LAURENCE (LAURIE): the boy next door, likes Jo, but marries Amy
[3]**MR. LAURENCE:** Laurie's grandfather, a rich old man
[3]**JOHN BROOKE:** Laurie's tutor and (later) Meg's husband
[1]**AUNT CARROL:** takes Amy to Europe
[2]**FRIEDRICH BHAER:** kind professor and (later) Jo's husband

The same actors can play the following parts:
[1]MARMEE and AUNT CARROL
[2]MR. MARCH and FRIEDRICH BHAER
[3]MR. LAURENCE and JOHN BROOKE

ACT 1 SCENE 1

(enter JO, MEG, BETH, and AMY)

JO: Christmas won't be Christmas without any presents!

MEG: It's so dreadful to be poor!

AMY: I don't think it's fair for some girls to have plenty of things, and other girls nothing at all.

BETH: *(happily)* We've got Father, Mother, and each other! What else could we POSSIBLY want! *(JO, MEG, and AMY all roll their eyes and sigh)*

JO: *(to audience, pointing at sisters)* That's Beth. She's the good sister. That's Meg, the oldest, and that's Amy, the youngest, and I'm Jo. So now you're all caught up.

(enter MARMEE)

MARCH SISTERS: Marmee!

JO: *(to audience)* Anybody can be called "mom." Only superstar moms are called "Marmee."

MARMEE: Girls! I have a letter from your father who has been away at war! *(reads letter)* Give them all of my dear love and a kiss. Remind them to be good so that when I come back to them I may be fonder and prouder than ever of my little women.

BETH: Of course we will, Marmee!

MARMEE: Speaking of being good, I know it's Christmas and we're poor, but there's a much poorer family down the street and I think we should give them our breakfast!

(pause; they all look at each other)

MARCH SISTERS: Um, sure...

MARMEE: Great! Let's pack up our delicious Christmas breakfast. Hooray!

MARCH SISTERS: *(not very excited)* Yeah... hooray.

(ALL exit)

ACT 1 SCENE 2

(enter JO and MEG)

MEG: Please be cool at this party, Jo. Hold your shoulder straight, and take short steps, and don't shake hands if you are introduced to anyone. It isn't the thing.

JO: Fine! So, which shoulder should I hold straight, left or right?

MEG: *(glares at JO)* And DON'T BE RUDE!

JO: I feel so awkward at events like this!

MEG: I'm going to dance with my friends. Be good, Jo. *(MEG runs to the corner of the stage and begins dancing)*

(enter LAURIE, walking slowly backward, looking overwhelmed; he bumps into JO)

JO: Oh!

LAURIE: Sorry! Wait! You live near my grandpa and me, don't you?

JO: Um, yeah. Next door. You're Mr. Laurence, right? I'm Jo.

LAURIE: I'm not Mr. Laurence, I'm only Laurie.

JO: Laurie Laurence, what an odd name. *(pause)* Whoops! That was rude, wasn't it?

MEG: *(calls from across the stage)* Yep! That was rude!

JO: *(under breath)* Fiddlesticks! *(to Laurie)* Why do you live with your grandpa?

LAURIE: My parents are dead.

JO: Bummer. Want to be best friends forever and ever?

LAURIE: Yes, I do!

JO: Fantastic!

(ALL exit)

ACT 1 SCENE 3

(enter JO, MEG, and AMY; there are a bunch of papers on the floor)

AMY: Girls, where are you going?

JO: Never mind. Little girls shouldn't ask questions.

AMY: WHAT?!

MEG: We're going to see a play with Laurie.

JO: And you can't come, 'cause you're a little girl!

AMY: Am not!

JO: Too bad, so sad! Farewell, baby Amy! *(JO and MEG exit quickly)*

AMY: *(calls after them)* You'll be sorry for this, Jo March, see if you ain't! What's this? *(she picks up the bunch of papers dramatically and exits as MEG and JO reenter)*

MEG: Wow, what a great play!

JO: Yep! Wait! *(looks around)* Where is my book? The one I JUST wrote? You know, the papers that were right here? *(points to floor)*

(enter AMY looking suspicious)

JO: Amy, you've got it!

AMY: You'll never see your silly old book again! I burned it up! "Little girls" can play with fire, you know. Muahahahahaha!

JO: *(screams)* Noooooooooooooooooooooooooo! That was the only copy in the world! It was my masterpiece! I'll never forgive you as long as I live.

(enter MARMEE)

MARMEE: *(to JO)* My dear, don't let the sun go down upon your anger. Forgive each other, and begin again tomorrow.

JO: She doesn't deserve to be forgiven. Do you even realize how hard it is living up to your expectations, Marmee? Man! Parents' expectations can be brutal! I'm outta here. I'm going ice-skating with Laurie. He gets me.

(JO begins walking across the stage with AMY sneaking behind her; MARMEE and MEG exit; LAURIE enters and links arms with JO; they begin "skating" around the stage, laughing)

LAURIE: *(to JO)* Stay away from the middle; the ice is thin!

(JO notices AMY "skating" across the stage)

JO: *(to audience)* If I weren't so mad at her, I'd warn her about the thin ice. But she's the one who wanted to play with fire! *(mimicking AMY's evil laugh)* Muahahahaha indeed!

(AMY falls dramatically to the floor)

AMY: Help! I fell through the ice! I'm drowning! And freezing! It's so coooooooold!

(JO and LAURIE rush over and pull AMY up; AMY coughs and shudders)

JO: This is all my fault! It's my dreadful temper! I could have warned her, and I didn't!

(enter MARMEE)

MARMEE: Don't worry. Amy will be fine.

AMY: *(gives a really shaky thumb's up)* Tot-tal-YYYYYYY.

MARMEE: *(to JO)* But that temper of yours needs to be controlled.

JO: I will try, Mother, I truly will. But you must help me, remind me, and keep me from flying out!

MARMEE: No problem! That's what mothers are for!

(ALL exit)

ACT 1 SCENE 4

(enter LAURIE, JO, MEG, BETH, AMY, and JOHN)

LAURIE: What a beautiful day for a picnic! Welcome to Camp Laurence!

AMY: So, what should we do?

JO: We could put on a play!

MEG: Uh, Jo… we're IN a play. *(motions to audience)* And we don't need to do the "play within a play" thing. This isn't Shakespeare.

JO: Fine.

MEG: Truth or dare?

BETH: Oh, we couldn't! It wouldn't be proper!

AMY: You're so boring, Beth.

LAURIE: John, you're my tutor, can't you think of something?

JOHN: Well, I am super smart! I know! Meg, do you want to practice your German?

MEG: Me? Now? Sure, I guess so… *(she begins counting in German)* Eins, zwei, drei, vier…

AMY: This is the worst picnic ever.

LAURIE: *(whispers loudly to JO)* John totally has a crush on Meg!

JO: How do you know?

LAURIE: He's been keeping one of her gloves in his pocket! I catch him looking at it ALL the time. Isn't that romantic?

JO: No, it's horrid! What is he, some kind of stalker? I wish you hadn't told me! I don't want anybody to take Meg away from me. Ugh, this day is ruined; have fun at your picnic without me! *(JO exits and everyone else shrugs and follows her offstage)*

MEG: Told you we should have played Truth or Dare!

ACT 1 SCENE 5

(enter JO, MEG, BETH, AMY, and LAURIE; entire scene is to audience)

LAURIE: And now, to lighten the mood...

ALL: Presenting: Our castles in the air!

LAURIE: Otherwise known as our hopes and dreams for the future.

MEG: I should like a lovely house... and heaps of money!

AMY: I want to be the best artist in the whole world! *(holds up stick figure drawing)*

JO: And I want to do something heroic or wonderful that won't be forgotten after I'm dead. I think I shall write books, and get rich and famous.

LAURIE: I want to be a famous musician! *(strums a few painful chords on a guitar)*

(ALL CHARACTERS turn and look at BETH)

BETH: I want to stay at home safe with Father and Mother, and help take care of the family.

JO: And that's why she's the good one.

LAURIE: Only the good die young, Beth.

JO: *(to LAURIE, while pointing at audience)* Shhhhh! No spoilers! Don't ruin it for them!

LAURIE: *(to audience)* Sorry. *(whispers)* Not sorry.

(JO pushes LAURIE offstage grumbling under her breath; ALL exit)

ACT 1 SCENE 6

(enter JO, MEG, BETH, and AMY)

MEG: While Marmee's out of town, we are supposed to go help that poor family again, remember?

BETH: I'll do it! I love helping people! *(BETH exits)*

JO: So, I was thinking about a new story I could write about…

(enter BETH, stumbling around)

BETH: The poor family has scarlet fever! Their baby died! And now I have scarlet fever! *(she falls dramatically to the ground)*

AMY: Oh no! This is awful!

MEG: *(feels BETH'S forehead)* I don't think she's going to make it!

JO: No! We are only halfway through the play, she can't die… yet!

MEG: I wish I had no heart, it aches so!

AMY: *(pushes MEG out of the way feels BETH'S forehead)* Wait! She's definitely going to live… for now!

MEG & JO: Hooray!

BETH: I'm better now, but I have the strangest feeling that I'll never be quite as healthy as I was before…

AMY: This is no time for doom and gloom! Let's go celebrate!

(ALL exit)

ACT 1 SCENE 7

(enter MR. MARCH)

MR. MARCH: *(to audience)* Hi! I'm the dad. I've been away as a chaplain in the civil war. You've heard of it, right? Anyway, it's Christmas time again, and I'm home and I just wanted to be polite and introduce myself. Carry on.

(exits)

ACT 1 SCENE 8

(enter JOHN and MEG)

JOHN: Meg, are you afraid of me or something? I hope you're not because I totally love you!

MEG: I'm too young to get married, John!

JOHN: I'll wait for you forever!

MEG: Seriously, forever?

JOHN: Forever!

MEG: Kinda creepy, but ok!

(enter AUNT MARCH; AUNT MARCH periodically throws money around while she talks)

AUNT MARCH: There's mischief going on, and I insist upon knowing what it is! Wait! You're not going to marry this poor man, are you, Meg?

MEG: Aunt March! What are you doing here? How is this even your business?

AUNT MARCH: You cannot marry this lowly tutor. If you do, not one penny of my money ever goes to you!

MEG: Excuse me? I shall marry whom I please, Aunt March, and you can leave your money to anyone you like.

AUNT MARCH: Then I'm done with you forever! Goodbye! *(AUNT MARCH exits)*

MEG: *(to JOHN)* I guess I do love you! But I still can't get married yet!

JOHN: That's okay, watch this! *(snaps fingers; someone crosses stage carrying a sign that says THREE YEARS LATER)* Ta-da! I told you... forever!

MEG: Perfect, let's go get hitched! *(they exit)*

ACT 2 SCENE 1

(enter JO, MEG, BETH, AMY, MARMEE, and MR. MARCH)

JO: Guess what everybody? I wrote a silly, romance-adventure story and it's going to be published, and they gave me a hundred dollars! That's like 3,000 dollars today!

BETH: That's amazing!

MARMEE: Good job, Jo!

MR. MARCH: A sensationalist story? Hmm. You can do better than this Jo. Aim at the highest, and never mind the money.

AMY: I think the money is the best part of it.

JO: I see your point, dad, but now I can send Beth and Mother to the seaside so Beth can feel better and not die like we are alluding to. See how generous I am? Now, I'm going to write a novel!

MR. MARCH: Make it metaphysical!

MARMEE: Don't put too much description in it!

MEG: Don't forget to add some tragedy!

AMY: And don't make it too fun!

JO: Right. Thanks for the advice, everyone!

BETH: I should like to see it printed soon!

JO: Me too, Beth, me too!

BETH: Preferably by page 55, because, well... you know... *(makes a "dead" looking face)*

JO: Page 55, got it!

(ALL exit)

ACT 2 SCENE 2

(enter JO, AMY, AUNT MARCH, and AUNT CARROL; once again, AUNT MARCH periodically throws money around while she talks)

JO: *(to AUNT CARROL)* Who are you?

AUNT CARROL: Um, I'm your Aunt Carrol. So tell me, girls, who is the nicer sister?

(AMY and JO look at each other)

AMY: I am.

JO: She is.

AUNT MARCH: *(to AUNT CARROL)* I told you so.

AUNT CARROL: Hmm, okay. And do either of you speak French?

AMY: Oui! Oo la la!

JO: Don't know a word. I'm very stupid about studying anything, can't bear French, It's such a slippery, silly sort of language.

AUNT CARROL: Well then, since Jo hates French, I'll take Amy to Europe with me as my young companion. Want to go?

AMY: Is that even a question? YES! Or should I say, bien sûr!

JO: Oh my tongue! My abominable tongue! Why can't I keep my big mouth shut!

AUNT MARCH: Maybe someday you'll learn, dear. But, I doubt it. Bye, Bye!

(ALL exit)

ACT 2 SCENE 3

(enter JO and LAURIE)

JO: So, Laurie, how many girls have you sent flowers to this week?

LAURIE: Nobody. Yet...

JO: Mother doesn't approve of flirting even in fun, and you do flirt desperately, Laurie.

LAURIE: Because it's fun! Jo, you should try it sometime.

JO: I really don't know how.

LAURIE: Take lessons of Amy, she has a regular talent for it.

JO: Laurie, all this flirting talk is making me really uncomfortable. *(to audience)* I think he's beginning to "LIKE me" like me. Instead of just like me. *(to LAURIE)* Look, I have no time to learn how to flirt since I'll be moving to New York right away.

LAURIE: It won't do a bit of good, Jo. My eye is on you, so mind what you do, or I'll come and bring you home.

JO: You'll do no such thing. Look, the big city is calling me, so good luck and goodbye!

(JO and LAURIE exit in different directions)

ACT 2 SCENE 4

(enter JO)

JO: *(to audience)* Here I am living in New York, just like a real writer! I live in a boarding house with some sweet families and this super cool German professor, Friedrich Bhaer... *(enter BHAER)*

BHAER: *(with German accent)* Hallo, Jo. So, you peep at me, I peep at you, and this is not bad, but see, I am not pleasanting when I say, haf you a wish for German?

JO: Excuse me?

BHAER: Would you like me to teach you German? Please say ja. That's yes. First lesson! *(offers JO a high five; JO ignores him)*

JO: *(to audience)* What is with all the men in this play offering to teach us girls German? *(to BHAER)* Sure, why not? But this isn't, like, a date, right? Because you have to be at least forty. That's really old.

BHAER: Ha! Well, let's just say I'm young at heart. Come on; we have a lot of work to do!

(JO and BHAER exit)

ACT 2 SCENE 5

(enter JO)

JO: *(to audience)* And just like that, the year is over and I'm back home! New York was fun, and I'll miss my good friend, Professor Bhaer, but my family needs me here.

(enter LAURIE)

LAURIE: Jo! Thank goodness you're home. I've missed you so much this past year! I have something super important to ask you…

JO: No, Laurie. Please don't!

LAURIE: You don't even know what I'm going to say! Look, Jo. I've loved you ever since I've known you. Will you marry me, pretty please?

JO: See, I knew what you were going to say. *(to audience)* Boys are so predictable.

LAURIE: Well?

JO: Nein.

LAURIE: Nine?

JO: No… NEIN. It's German for NO. You're my best friend. It would be so weird!

LAURIE: Hold on. You love that old man, don't you? The *(air quotes)* "professor?"

JO: No, I don't! *(to audience)* Wait… do I? Oh man, I might.

LAURIE: I'm so sad! *(starts melodramatically crying)*

(enter MR. LAURENCE)

MR. LAURENCE: Let's go to Europe, my boy! Travel makes everything better!

LAURIE: Nothing can fix my broken, mutilated, utterly destroyed heart! But Europe does sound cool. Thanks, Grandpa. At least SOMEBODY loves me. *(glares at JO)*

(ALL exit)

ACT 2 SCENE 6

(enter JO and BETH)

JO: You look terrible, Beth.

BETH: I never really got over that bout of scarlet fever. I think I need another trip to the seashore.

JO: Let's do it! *(they link arms and skip around stage)* Ahhhhhhhhhhh, the ocean air! So fresh! And *(sniffs the air)*... fishy. And sort of stinky, but...

BETH: Listen, Jo, I looked ahead in the play, and I'm going to die soon.

JO: What? NO! Beth, you must get well!

BETH: I want to! But, you know, I can't change the plot!

JO: Well, the plot is dumb.

BETH: Can't argue with you there. Let's just enjoy the time we have left, shall we?

JO: You're too good for this world, Beth.

BETH: I know, Jo. I know.

(ALL exit)

ACT 2 SCENE 7

(enter MEG and JOHN; MEG is holding two dolls)

JOHN: I love our babies, Meg, but I miss my wife! You're always taking care of them!

MEG: Well, you're always gone! Maybe you should hang out at home some time!

(enter MARMEE)

MARMEE: Trouble in paradise? May I offer some advice?

MEG: Sure, Marmee.

MARMEE: *(sweetly)* Don't neglect husband for children, don't shut him out of the nursery, but teach him how to help in it. His place is there as well as yours, and the children need him.

MEG: Soooo, equal rights. Okay. Anything else?

MARMEE: Yes! I have a whole bunch of advice for you on how to be a happily married couple in the late 1800s!

JOHN: We're all ears, Marmee!

MEG: Yes, Marmee, show us the way!

(MARMEE talking to them as they exit)

ACT 2 SCENE 8

(enter AMY and LAURIE from opposite sides of the stage)

AMY: Laurie?!

LAURIE: Amy! Bonjour! Fancy meeting you over here in France.

AMY: *(to audience)* He's looking good!

LAURIE: *(to audience)* Wow! She's all grown up! And so pretty!

(they look at each other and giggle)

LAURIE: How about we row this boat around the lake?

AMY: Let's do it!

(they sit side-by-side onstage and mime rowing a boat, perfectly in sync)

AMY: How well we pull together, don't we?

LAURIE: So well that I wish we might always pull in the same boat. Get it?

AMY: Are you saying we should get married?

LAURIE: Yep!

AMY: *(to audience)* Yes, I know he proposed to my sister first. Don't judge. He's dreamy! *(to LAURIE)* I'm in!

(they high five and exit)

ACT 2 SCENE 9

(enter JO, MEG, JOHN, MARMEE, MR. MARCH, and BETH; BETH lies down onstage and everyone else gathers around her)

BETH: Well everyone, it's time for me to go.

(ALL CHARACTERS are crying or sniffling)

MEG: This is terrible!

MARMEE: My baby!

BETH: I love you all! And remember... love is the only thing we can carry with us when we go, and it makes the end so easy!

(BETH dies melodramatically; ALL characters wail and cry; Beth gets up and twirls herself offstage while the rest of the characters wave to her and blow her kisses)

MR. MARCH: She'll always be our angel!!

JO: *(to audience)* Louisa May Alcott. Making readers cry since 1868.

(ALL exit)

ACT 2 SCENE 10

(enter JO)

JO: *(to audience)* An old maid, that's what I'm to be. A literary spinster, with a pen for a spouse! I mean, I'm almost twenty-five! Ugh!

(enter BHAER)

BHAER: Hallo, Jo!

JO: What are you doing here?

BHAER: Oh, you know, I was just… conveniently passing through your town…

JO: Well, I'm always glad to see you, sir.

BHAER: I got a new job, and I'm moving to the West.

JO: Congratulations, but unfortunately, you can't go… because I love you!

BHAER: Now I will haf to show thee all my heart, and I so gladly will, because thou must take care of it hereafter! That means I love you, too!

JO: You're SO romantic! I don't even care that you're old!

BHAER: Just like stinky cheese, I get better with age!

(JO and BHAER stay on stage)

ACT 2 SCENE 11

(AUNT MARCH enters)

AUNT MARCH: I'm very old and it's time for me to die. But I wanted to let you know I'm leaving you my house! *(she hands JO a set of keys and then dies)*

JO: Aunt March! *(looks down at AUNT MARCH on the floor)* Um, thank you? *(steps over body, to BHAER)* I know what we can do with that big old house! I want to open a school for little lads—a good, happy, homelike school! And you can teach them!

BHAER: That I can do!

(enter MEG, JOHN, AMY, LAURIE, and MARMEE)

MARMEE: Oh, my girls, however long you may live, I never can wish you a greater happiness than this!

MEG: *(to audience)* By "this," Marmee means domestic life.

AMY: Right! We all end up with husbands, houses, and children. Oh, and laundry. So much laundry.

JO: But where's the intrigue! The scandal! The adventure!

LAURIE: *(interrupting)* Oh, come on, Jo. You've gotta know your audience. People like happy endings.

JO: *(to audience)* Well. I'd love to offer you a more exciting ending than "they all lived happily ever after," but hey, that's all she wrote. Literally. Until the sequel anyway...

LAURIE: Wait. There's a sequel?

BETH: *(pops her head onstage)* It's called Little Men. *(whispers dramatically)* Not as popular.

BHAER: Looks like we have some work to do, boys!

MEG: And on that note...

ALL: *(with bravado)* THE END!

(ALL CHARACTERS wave goodbye to the audience and exit)

NOTES

The 25-Minute or so Little Women for Kids
by Louisa May Alcott
Creatively modified by Khara C. Barnhart
and Brendan P. Kelso
13-16 Actors

CAST OF CHARACTERS:

JOSEPHINE MARCH (JO): aspiring writer and sarcastically snarky

MARGARET MARCH (MEG): the oldest March sister

BETH MARCH: another March sister, quiet and sweet, ALWAYS nice

AMY MARCH: the youngest March sister

MARMEE: the March sisters' mom

[1]**MR. MARCH:** the March sisters' dad

AUNT MARCH: grumpy aunt of the March sisters

[2]**HANNAH:** the March family's servant, doesn't talk much

THE REST...

THEODORE LAURENCE (LAURIE): the boy next door, likes Jo, but marries Amy

[1]**MR. LAURENCE:** Laurie's grandfather, a rich old man

[3]**JOHN BROOKE:** Laurie's tutor and (later) Meg's husband

SALLIE: Meg's friend

[3]**DOCTOR:** the doctor

[2]**AUNT CARROL:** takes Amy to Europe

FRIEDRICH BHAER: kind professor and (later) Jo's husband

ESTHER: Aunt March's maid (non-speaking role)

The same actors can play the following parts:
[1] MR. MARCH and MR. LAURENCE
[2] HANNAH and AUNT CARROL
[3] JOHN BROOKE and DOCTOR

ACT 1 SCENE 1

(enter JO, MEG, BETH, and AMY)

JO: Christmas won't be Christmas without any presents!

MEG: It's so dreadful to be poor!

AMY: I don't think it's fair for some girls to have plenty of things, and other girls nothing at all.

BETH: *(happily)* We've got Father, Mother, and each other! What else could we POSSIBLY want! *(JO, MEG, and AMY all roll their eyes and sigh)*

JO: *(to audience, pointing at sisters)* That's Beth. She's the good sister. That's Meg, the oldest, and that's Amy, the youngest, and I'm Jo. So now you're all caught up.

(enter MARMEE)

MARCH SISTERS: Marmee!

JO: *(to audience)* Anybody can be called "mom." Only superstar moms are called "Marmee."

MARMEE: Girls! I have a letter from your father who has been away at war! *(reads letter)* Give them all of my dear love and a kiss. Remind them to be good so that when I come back to them I may be fonder and prouder than ever of my little women.

BETH: Of course we will, Marmee!

MARMEE: Speaking of being good, I know it's Christmas and we're poor, but there's a much poorer family down the street and I think we should give them our breakfast!

(pause; they all look at each other)

MARCH SISTERS: Um, sure...

MARMEE: Great! *(calls offstage)* Hannah?!

(enter HANNAH)

HANNAH: Yes, ma'am.

MARMEE: *(to HANNAH)* Pack up our delicious Christmas breakfast! We are giving it away! Hooray!

MARCH SISTERS: *(not very excited)* Yeah... hooray.

HANNAH: Yes, ma'am.

(ALL exit)

ACT 1 SCENE 2

(enter JO and MEG)

MEG: Please be cool at this party, Jo. Hold your shoulder straight, and take short steps, and don't shake hands if you are introduced to anyone. It isn't the thing.

JO: Fine! So, which shoulder should I hold straight, left or right?

MEG: *(glares at JO)* And DON'T BE RUDE!

JO: I feel so awkward at events like this! *(enter SALLIE)* Hey, there's Sallie!

SALLIE: Meg! Jo! Are you ready to par-tay? Whoop Whoop! *(she begins dancing and MEG joins her; they run to a corner of the stage and continue dancing)*

(enter LAURIE, walking slowly backward, looking overwhelmed; he bumps into JO)

JO: Oh!

LAURIE: Sorry! Wait! You live near my grandpa and me, don't you?

JO: Um, yeah. Next door. You're Mr. Laurence, right? I'm Jo.

LAURIE: I'm not Mr. Laurence, I'm only Laurie.

JO: Laurie Laurence, what an odd name. *(pause)* Whoops! That was rude, wasn't it?

MEG: *(calls from across the stage)* Yep! That was rude!

JO: *(under breath)* Fiddlesticks! *(to Laurie)* Why do you live with your grandpa?

LAURIE: My parents are dead.

JO: Bummer. Want to be best friends forever and ever?

LAURIE: Yes, I do!

JO: Fantastic!

(ALL exit)

ACT 1 SCENE 3

(enter JO, MEG, and AMY; there are a bunch of papers on the floor)

AMY: Girls, where are you going?

JO: Never mind. Little girls shouldn't ask questions.

AMY: WHAT?!

MEG: We're going to see a play with Laurie.

JO: And you can't come, 'cause you're a little girl!

AMY: Am not!

JO: Too bad, so sad! Farewell, baby Amy! *(JO and MEG exit quickly)*

AMY: *(calls after them)* You'll be sorry for this, Jo March, see if you ain't! What's this? *(she picks up the bunch of papers dramatically and exits as MEG and JO reenter)*

MEG: Wow, what a great play!

JO: Yep! Wait! *(looks around)* Where is my book? The one I JUST wrote? You know, the papers that were right here? *(points to floor)*

(enter AMY looking suspicious)

JO: Amy, you've got it!

AMY: You'll never see your silly old book again! I burned it up! "Little girls" can play with fire, you know. Muahahahahaha!

JO: *(screams)* Noooooooooooooooooooooooooo! That was the only copy in the world! It was my masterpiece! I'll never forgive you as long as I live.

(enter MARMEE)

MARMEE: *(to JO)* My dear, don't let the sun go down upon your anger. Forgive each other, and begin again tomorrow.

JO: She doesn't deserve to be forgiven. Do you even realize how hard it is living up to your expectations, Marmee? Man! Parents' expectations can be brutal! I'm outta here. I'm going ice-skating with Laurie. He gets me.

(JO begins walking across the stage with AMY sneaking behind her; MARMEE and MEG exit; LAURIE enters and links arms with JO; they begin "skating" around the stage, laughing)

LAURIE: *(to JO)* Stay away from the middle; the ice is thin!

(JO notices AMY "skating" across the stage)

JO: *(to audience)* If I weren't so mad at her, I'd warn her about the thin ice. But she's the one who wanted to play with fire! *(mimicking AMY's evil laugh)* Muahahahaha indeed!

(AMY falls dramatically to the floor)

AMY: Help! I fell through the ice! I'm drowning! And freezing! It's so coooooooold!

(JO and LAURIE rush over and pull AMY up; AMY coughs and shudders)

JO: This is all my fault! It's my dreadful temper! I could have warned her, and I didn't!

(enter MARMEE)

MARMEE: Don't worry. Amy will be fine.

AMY: *(gives a really shaky thumb's up)* Tot-tal-yyyyyyy.

MARMEE: *(to JO)* But that temper of yours needs to be controlled.

JO: I will try, Mother, I truly will. But you must help me, remind me, and keep me from flying out!

MARMEE: No problem! That's what mothers are for!

(ALL exit)

ACT 1 SCENE 4

(enter LAURIE, JO, MEG, BETH, AMY, JOHN, and SALLIE)

LAURIE: What a beautiful day for a picnic! Welcome to Camp Laurence!

SALLIE: I'm up for fun and games as long as my dress doesn't get dirty!

AMY: So, what should we do?

JO: We could put on a play!

MEG: Uh, Jo... we're IN a play. *(motions to audience)* And we don't need to do the "play within a play" thing. This isn't Shakespeare.

JO: Fine.

SALLIE: Truth or dare?

BETH: Oh, we couldn't! It wouldn't be proper!

AMY: You're so boring, Beth.

LAURIE: John, you're my tutor, can't you think of something?

JOHN: Well, I am super smart! I know! Meg, do you want to practice your German?

MEG: Me? Now? Sure, I guess so... *(she begins counting in German)* Eins, zwei, drei, vier...

SALLIE: This is the worst picnic ever.

LAURIE: *(whispers loudly to JO)* John totally has a crush on Meg!

JO: How do you know?

LAURIE: He's been keeping one of her gloves in his pocket! I catch him looking at it ALL the time. Isn't that romantic?

JO: No, it's horrid! What is he, some kind of stalker? I wish you hadn't told me! I don't want anybody to take Meg away from me. Ugh, this day is ruined; have fun at your picnic without me! *(JO exits and everyone else shrugs and follows her offstage)*

SALLIE: Told you we should have played Truth or Dare!

ACT 1 SCENE 5

(enter JO, MEG, BETH, AMY, and LAURIE; entire scene is to audience)

LAURIE: And now, to lighten the mood...

ALL: Presenting: Our castles in the air!

LAURIE: Otherwise known as our hopes and dreams for the future.

MEG: I should like a lovely house... and heaps of money!

AMY: I want to be the best artist in the whole world! *(holds up stick figure drawing)*

JO: And I want to do something heroic or wonderful that won't be forgotten after I'm dead. I think I shall write books, and get rich and famous.

LAURIE: I want to be a famous musician! *(strums a few painful chords on a guitar)*

(ALL CHARACTERS turn and look at BETH)

BETH: I want to stay at home safe with Father and Mother, and help take care of the family.

JO: And that's why she's the good one.

LAURIE: Only the good die young, Beth.

JO: *(to LAURIE, while pointing at audience)* Shhhhh! No spoilers! Don't ruin it for them!

LAURIE: *(to audience)* Sorry. *(whispers)* Not sorry.

(JO pushes LAURIE offstage grumbling under her breath; ALL exit)

ACT 1 SCENE 6

(enter JO, MEG, BETH, and AMY)

MEG: While Marmee's out of town, we are supposed to go help that poor family again, remember?

BETH: I'll do it! I love helping people! *(BETH exits)*

JO: So, I was thinking about a new story I could write about...

(enter BETH, stumbling around)

BETH: The poor family has scarlet fever! Their baby died! And now I have scarlet fever! *(she falls dramatically to the ground)*

AMY: Oh no! This is awful!

(enter HANNAH and DOCTOR)

DOCTOR: *(feels BETH'S forehead)* I don't think she's going to make it!

HANNAH: No! We are only halfway through the play, she can't die... yet!

MEG: I wish I had no heart, it aches so!

DOCTOR: *(feels BETH'S forehead again)* Wait! I was wrong. She's going to live... for now!

MEG & JO: Hooray!

HANNAH: Wow, that was quick.

DOCTOR: Short play, gotta keep it moving!

BETH: I'm better now, but I have the strangest feeling that I'll never be quite as healthy as I was before...

AMY: This is no time for doom and gloom! Let's go celebrate!

(ALL exit)

ACT 1 SCENE 7

(enter MR. MARCH)

MR. MARCH: *(to audience)* Hi! I'm the dad. I've been away as a chaplain in the civil war. You've heard of it, right? Anyway, it's Christmas time again, and I'm home and I just wanted to be polite and introduce myself. Carry on.

(he exits)

ACT 1 SCENE 8

(enter JOHN and MEG)

JOHN: Meg, are you afraid of me or something? I hope you're not because I totally love you!

MEG: I'm too young to get married, John!

JOHN: I'll wait for you forever!

MEG: Seriously, forever?

JOHN: Forever!

MEG: Kinda creepy, but ok!

(enter AUNT MARCH and ESTHER; AUNT MARCH periodically throws money around while she talks, and ESTHER stays busy constantly cleaning up the money)

AUNT MARCH: There's mischief going on, and I insist upon knowing what it is! Wait! You're not going to marry this poor man, are you, Meg?

MEG: Aunt March! What are you doing here? How is this even your business?

AUNT MARCH: You cannot marry this lowly tutor. If you do, not one penny of my money ever goes to you!

MEG: Excuse me? I shall marry whom I please, Aunt March, and you can leave your money to anyone you like.

AUNT MARCH: Then I'm done with you forever! Goodbye! *(AUNT MARCH and ESTHER exit)*

MEG: *(to JOHN)* I guess I do love you! But I still can't get married yet!

JOHN: That's okay, watch this! *(snaps fingers; enter ESTHER carrying a sign that says THREE YEARS LATER; she holds it up, crosses the stage, and exits)* Ta-da! I told you... forever!

MEG: Perfect, let's go get hitched!

(they exit)

ACT 2 SCENE 1

(enter JO, MEG, BETH, AMY, MARMEE, and MR. MARCH)

JO: Guess what everybody? I wrote a silly, romance-adventure story and it's going to be published, and they gave me a hundred dollars! That's like 3,000 dollars today!

BETH: That's amazing!

MARMEE: Good job, Jo!

MR. MARCH: A sensationalist story? Hmm. You can do better than this Jo. Aim at the highest, and never mind the money.

AMY: I think the money is the best part of it.

JO: I see your point, dad, but now I can send Beth and Mother to the seaside so Beth can feel better and not die like we are alluding to. See how generous I am? Now, I'm going to write a novel!

MR. MARCH: Make it metaphysical!

MARMEE: Don't put too much description in it!

MEG: Don't forget to add some tragedy!

AMY: And don't make it too fun!

JO: Right. Thanks for the advice, everyone!

BETH: I should like to see it printed soon!

JO: Me too, Beth, me too!

BETH: Preferably by page 85, because, well... you know... *(makes a "dead" looking face)*

JO: Page 85, got it!

(ALL exit)

ACT 2 SCENE 2

(enter JO, AMY, AUNT MARCH, ESTHER, and AUNT CARROL; once again, AUNT MARCH periodically throws money around while she talks, and ESTHER stays busy constantly cleaning up the money)

JO: *(to AUNT CARROL)* Who are you?

AUNT CARROL: Um, I'm your Aunt Carrol. So tell me, girls, who is the nicer sister?

(AMY and JO look at each other)

AMY: I am.

JO: She is.

AUNT MARCH: *(to AUNT CARROL)* I told you so.

AUNT CARROL: Hmm, okay. And do either of you speak French?

AMY: Oui! Oo la la!

JO: Don't know a word. I'm very stupid about studying anything, can't bear French, it's such a slippery, silly sort of language.

AUNT CARROL: Well then, since Jo hates French, I'll take Amy to Europe with me as my young companion. Want to go?

AMY: Is that even a question? YES! Or should I say, bien sûr!

JO: Oh my tongue! My abominable tongue! Why can't I keep my big mouth shut!

AUNT MARCH: Maybe someday you'll learn, dear. But, I doubt it. Bye, Bye!

(ALL exit)

ACT 2 SCENE 3

(enter JO and LAURIE)

JO: So, Laurie, how many girls have you sent flowers to this week?

LAURIE: Nobody. Yet...

JO: Mother doesn't approve of flirting even in fun, and you do flirt desperately, Laurie.

LAURIE: Because it's fun! Jo, you should try it sometime.

JO: I really don't know how.

LAURIE: Take lessons of Amy, she has a regular talent for it.

JO: Laurie, all this flirting talk is making me really uncomfortable. *(to audience)* I think he's beginning to "LIKE me" like me. Instead of just like me. *(to LAURIE)* Look, I have no time to learn how to flirt since I'll be moving to New York right away.

LAURIE: It won't do a bit of good, Jo. My eye is on you, so mind what you do, or I'll come and bring you home.

JO: You'll do no such thing. Look, the big city is calling me, so good luck and goodbye!

(JO and LAURIE exit in different directions)

ACT 2 SCENE 4

(enter JO)

JO: *(to audience)* Here I am living in New York, just like a real writer! I live in a boarding house with some sweet families and this super cool German professor, Friedrich Bhaer... *(enter BHAER)*

BHAER: *(with German accent)* Hallo, Jo. So, you peep at me, I peep at you, and this is not bad, but see, I am not pleasanting when I say, haf you a wish for German?

JO: Excuse me?

BHAER: Would you like me to teach you German? Please say ja. That's yes. First lesson! *(offers JO a high five; JO ignores him)*

JO: *(to audience)* What is with all the men in this play offering to teach us girls German? *(to BHAER)* Sure, why not? But this isn't, like, a date, right? Because you have to be at least forty. That's really old.

BHAER: Ha! Well, let's just say I'm young at heart. Come on; we have a lot of work to do!

(JO and BHAER exit)

ACT 2 SCENE 5

(enter JO)

JO: *(to audience)* And just like that, the year is over and I'm back home! New York was fun, and I'll miss my good friend, Professor Bhaer, but my family needs me here.

(enter LAURIE)

LAURIE: Jo! Thank goodness you're home. I've missed you so much this past year! I have something super important to ask you...

JO: No, Laurie. Please don't!

LAURIE: You don't even know what I'm going to say! Look, Jo. I've loved you ever since I've known you. Will you marry me, pretty please?

JO: See, I knew what you were going to say. *(to audience)* Boys are so predictable.

LAURIE: Well?

JO: Nein.

LAURIE: Nine?

JO: No... NEIN. It's German for NO. You're my best friend. It would be so weird!

LAURIE: Hold on. You love that old man, don't you? The *(air quotes)* "professor?"

JO: No, I don't! *(to audience)* Wait... do I? Oh man, I might.

LAURIE: I'm so sad! *(starts melodramatically crying)*

(enter MR. LAURENCE)

MR. LAURENCE: Let's go to Europe, my boy! Travel makes everything better!

LAURIE: Nothing can fix my broken, mutilated, utterly destroyed heart! But Europe does sound cool. Thanks, Grandpa. At least SOMEBODY loves me. *(glares at JO)*

(ALL exit)

ACT 2 SCENE 6

(enter JO and BETH)

JO: You look terrible, Beth.

BETH: I never really got over that bout of scarlet fever. I think I need another trip to the seashore.

JO: Let's do it! *(they link arms and skip around stage)* Ahhhhhhhhhhh, the ocean air! So fresh! And *(sniffs the air)*... fishy. And sort of stinky, but...

BETH: Listen, Jo, I looked ahead in the play, and I'm going to die soon.

JO: What? NO! Beth, you must get well!

BETH: I want to! But, you know, I can't change the plot!

JO: Well, the plot is dumb.

BETH: Can't argue with you there. Let's just enjoy the time we have left, shall we?

JO: You're too good for this world, Beth.

BETH: I know, Jo. I know.

(ALL exit)

ACT 2 SCENE 7

(enter MEG and JOHN; MEG is holding two dolls)

JOHN: I love our babies, Meg, but I miss my wife! You're always taking care of them!

MEG: Well, you're always gone! Maybe you should hang out at home sometime!

(enter MARMEE)

MARMEE: Trouble in paradise? May I offer some advice?

MEG: Sure, Marmee.

MARMEE: *(sweetly)* Don't neglect husband for children, don't shut him out of the nursery, but teach him how to help in it. His place is there as well as yours, and the children need him.

MEG: Soooo, equal rights. Okay. Anything else?

MARMEE: Yes! I have a whole bunch of advice for you on how to be a happily married couple in the late 1800s!

JOHN: We're all ears, Marmee!

MEG: Yes, Marmee, show us the way!

(MARMEE talking to them as they exit)

ACT 2 SCENE 8

(enter AMY and LAURIE from opposite sides of the stage)

AMY: Laurie?!

LAURIE: Amy! Bonjour! Fancy meeting you over here in France.

AMY: *(to audience)* He's looking good!

LAURIE: *(to audience)* Wow! She's all grown up! And so pretty!

(they look at each other and giggle)

LAURIE: How about we row this boat around the lake?

AMY: Let's do it!

(they sit side-by-side onstage and mime rowing a boat, perfectly in sync)

AMY: How well we pull together, don't we?

LAURIE: So well that I wish we might always pull in the same boat. Get it?

AMY: Are you saying we should get married?

LAURIE: Yep!

AMY: *(to audience)* Yes, I know he proposed to my sister first. Don't judge. He's dreamy! *(to LAURIE)* I'm in! *(they high five and exit)*

ACT 2 SCENE 9

(enter JO, MEG, JOHN, MARMEE, MR. MARCH, HANNAH, and BETH; BETH lies down onstage and everyone else gathers around her)

BETH: Well everyone, it's time for me to go.

(ALL CHARACTERS are crying or sniffling)

MEG: This is terrible!

MARMEE: My baby!

BETH: I love you all! And remember... ==love is the only thing we can carry with us when we go, and it makes the end so easy!==

(BETH dies melodramatically; ALL characters wail and cry; Beth gets up and twirls herself offstage while the rest of the characters wave to her and blow her kisses)

HANNAH: She'll always be our angel!!

JO: *(to audience)* Louisa May Alcott. Making readers cry since 1868.

(ALL exit)

ACT 2 SCENE 10

(enter JO)

JO: *(to audience)* An old maid, that's what I'm to be. A literary spinster, with a pen for a spouse! I mean, I'm almost twenty-five! Ugh!

(enter BHAER)

BHAER: Hallo, Jo!

JO: What are you doing here?

BHAER: Oh, you know, I was just... conveniently passing through your town...

JO: Well, I'm always glad to see you, sir.

BHAER: I got a new job, and I'm moving to the West.

JO: Congratulations, but unfortunately, you can't go... because I love you!

BHAER: Now I will haf to show thee all my heart, and I so gladly will, because thou must take care of it hereafter! That means I love you, too!

JO: You're SO romantic! I don't even care that you're old!

BHAER: Just like stinky cheese, I get better with age!

(JO and BHAER exit)

ACT 2 SCENE 11

(enter JO, BHAER, AUNT MARCH, and ESTHER)

AUNT MARCH: I'm very old and it's time for me to die. But I wanted to let you know I'm leaving you my house! *(she dies; ESTHER hands JO a set of keys and exits)*

JO: Aunt March! *(looks down at AUNT MARCH on the floor)* Um, thank you? *(steps over body, to BHAER)* I know what we can do with that big old house! I want to open a school for little lads—a good, happy, homelike school! And you can teach them!

BHAER: That I can do!

(enter MEG, JOHN, AMY, LAURIE, MARMEE and MR. MARCH)

MARMEE: Oh, my girls, however long you may live, I never can wish you a greater happiness than this!

MEG: *(to audience)* By "this," Marmee means domestic life.

AMY: Right! We all end up with husbands, houses, and children. Oh, and laundry. So much laundry.

JO: But where's the intrigue! The scandal! The adventure!

LAURIE: *(interrupting)* Oh, come on, Jo. You've gotta know your audience. People like happy endings.

JO: *(to audience)* Well. I'd love to offer you a more exciting ending than "they all lived happily ever after," but hey, that's all she wrote. Literally. Until the sequel anyway…

LAURIE: Wait. There's a sequel?

BETH: *(pops her head onstage)* It's called Little Men. *(whispers dramatically)* Not as popular.

BHAER: Looks like we have some work to do, boys!

MEG: And on that note…

ALL: *(with bravado)* THE END!

(ALL CHARACTERS wave goodbye to the audience and exit)

Special Thanks

Special thanks to all our beta readers for Little Women for Kids. Their feedback is always amazingly helpful! Melissa G., Isidro R., Dave C., Angi Herrick, Roy R., Debbie P., Jerry M. and his 5th grade drama class (go Crespo!), Steffi, Amanda M., Emilia W., Debbie P., Angie A. and her girls, Bradley W., Holli W., and Lisa M.

And a big thank you to Khara for convincing me that Pride and Little Women were the right way to go!

-Brendan

Sneak Peeks at other Playing With Plays books:

Pride & Prejudice for Kids..Pg 91
King Lear for Kids...Pg 93
Christmas Carol for Kids...Pg 96
Two Gentlemen of Verona for Kids ....Pg 99
Alice in Wonderland for Kids..Pg 102

Sneak peek of
Pride & Prejudice for Kids

ACT 1 SCENE 2

(enter ELIZABETH, MARY, KITTY, LYDIA, MR. BENNET and MRS. BENNET)

MRS. BENNET: Well, girls, we certainly have had a lot of fun lately at all these dances.

MARY: And how strange, Lizzy, that Mr. Darcy keeps trying to dance with you after he insulted you. Maybe he likes you now!

(MR. DARCY pops his head onstage)

MR. DARCY: *(to audience)* It's true. *(melodramatic sigh)* I'm reluctantly forced to acknowledge her figure to be light and pleasing, and I am caught by her easy playfulness. In other words, Elizabeth Bennet is pretty and fun. Ugh! *(he returns offstage)*

ELIZABETH: Well I could never like him. And I'll never dance with him, so there!

LYDIA: Can we please talk about something more interesting?

KITTY: Like, the officers!

LYDIA: Oh, the officers! *(KITTY and LYDIA squeal)*

KITTY: So handsome!

LYDIA: So brave! *(they squeal again)*

MR. BENNET: From all that I can collect by your manner of talking, you must be two of the silliest girls in the country. I have suspected it some time, but I am now convinced.

(enter JANE)

JANE: Guess what! I've been invited to Mr. Bingley's house for a visit!

BENNET SISTERS: Ooooooo! He likes youuuuuuuuu!

MRS. BENNET: Better go on horseback, because it seems likely to rain; and then you must stay all night.

ELIZABETH: *(sarcastically)* Really? Solid plan, Mom.

JANE: Okay, bye! *(she exits)*

MARY: Hey, look, it's raining!

MRS. BENNET: Woot! My plan is working! *(starts dancing around in a victory dance; ALL exit)*

Sneak peek of
King Lear for Kids
ACT 1 SCENE 1
KING LEAR's palace

(enter FOOL entertaining the audience with jokes, dancing, juggling, Hula Hooping... whatever the actor's skill may be; enter KENT)

KENT: Hey, Fool!

FOOL: What did you call me?!

KENT: I called you Fool.

FOOL: That's my name, don't wear it out! *(to audience)* Seriously, that's my name in the play!

(enter LEAR, CORNWALL, ALBANY, GONERIL, REGAN, and CORDELIA)

LEAR: The lords of France and Burgundy are outside. They both want to marry you, Cordelia.

ALL: Ooooooo!

LEAR: *(to audience)* Between you and me she IS my favorite child! *(to the girls)* Daughters, I need to talk to you about something. It's a really big deal.

GONERIL & REGAN: Did you buy us presents?

LEAR: This is even better than presents!

GONERIL & REGAN: Goody, goody!!!

CORDELIA: Father, your love is enough for me.

LEAR: Give me the map there, Kent. Girls, I'm tired. I've made a decision: Know that we - and by 'we' I mean 'me' - have divided in three our kingdom...

KENT: Whoa! Sir, dividing the kingdom may cause

chaos! People could die!

FOOL: Well, this IS a tragedy...

LEAR: You worry too much, Kent. I'm giving it to my daughters so their husbands can be rich and powerful... like me!

CORNWALL & ALBANY: Sweet!

GONERIL & REGAN: Wait... what?

CORDELIA: This is olden times. That means that everything we own belongs to our husbands.

GONERIL & REGAN: Olden times stink!

CORDELIA: Truth.

LEAR: So, my daughters, tell your daddy how much you love him. Goneril, our eldest-born, speak first.

GONERIL: Sir, I love you more than words can say! More than outer space, puppies and cotton candy! I love you more than any child has ever loved a father in the history of the entire world, dearest Pops!

CORDELIA: *(to audience)* Holy moly! Surely, he won't be fooled by that. *(to self)* Love, and be silent.

LEAR: Thanks, sweetie! I'm giving you this big chunk of the kingdom here. What says our second daughter, Our dearest Regan, wife to Cornwall? Speak.

REGAN: What she said, Daddy... times a thousand!

CORDELIA: *(to audience)* What?! I love my father more than either of them. But I can't express it in words. My love's more richer than my tongue.

LEAR: Wow, Regan! You get this big hunk of the kingdom. Cordelia, what can you tell me to get this giant piece of kingdom as your own? Speak.

CORDELIA: Nothing, my lord.

LEAR: Nothing?!?

CORDELIA: Nothing.

LEAR: Come on, now. Nothing will come of nothing.

CORDELIA: I love you as a daughter loves her father.

LEAR: Try a little, harder, sweetie!

CORDELIA: Why are my sisters married if they give you all their love?

LEAR: How did you get so mean?

CORDELIA: Father, I will not insult you by telling you my love is like... as big as a whale.

LEAR: *(getting mad)* Fine. I'll split your share between your sisters.

REGAN, GONERIL, & CORNWALL: Yessss!

KENT: Whoa! Let's all just calm down a minute!

LEAR: Peace, Kent! You don't want to mess with me right now. I told you she was my favorite...

GONERIL & REGAN: What!?

LEAR: ...and she can't even tell me she loves me more than a whale? Nope. Now I'm mad.

KENT: Royal Lear, really...

LEAR: Kent, I'm pretty emotional right now! You better not try to talk me out of this...

KENT: Sir, you're acting ... insane.

Sneak peek of
Christmas Carol for Kids

(enter GHOST PRESENT wearing a robe and holding a turkey leg and a goblet)

GHOST PRESENT: Wake up, Scrooge! I am the Ghost of Christmas Present. Look upon me!

SCROOGE: I'm looking. Not that impressed. But let's get on with it.

GHOST PRESENT: Touch my robe! *(SCROOGE touches GHOST PRESENT's robe. Pause. They look at each other)* Er...it must be broken. Guess we walk. Come on. *(they begin walking downstage)*

SCROOGE: Where are we going?

GHOST PRESENT: Your employee, Bob Cratchit's house. Oh look, here we are.

(enter BOB, MRS. CRATCHIT, MARTHA CRATCHIT, and TINY TIM, who has a crutch in one hand; they are all holding bowls)

BOB: *(to audience)* Hi, we're the Cratchit family. We are a REALLY happy family!

MRS. CRATCHIT: *(to audience)* Yes, but we're REALLY poor, too. Thanks to HIS boss! *(pointing at BOB)*

MARTHA: *(to audience)* Yeah, as you can see our bowls are empty. *(shows empty bowl)* We practically survive off air.

TINY TIM: *(to audience)* But we're happy!

MRS. CRATCHIT: *(to audience; overly sappy)* Because we have each other.

TINY TIM: And love!

SCROOGE: *(to GHOST PRESENT)* Seriously, are they for real?

GHOST PRESENT: Yep! Adorable, isn't it?

BOB: A merry Christmas to us all.

TINY TIM: God bless us every one!

SCROOGE: Spirit, tell me if Tiny Tim will live.

GHOST PRESENT: *(puts hands to head as if looking into the future)* Ooooo, not so good... I see a vacant seat in the poor chimney corner, and a crutch without an owner. If SOMEBODY doesn't change SOMETHING, the child will die.

SCROOGE: No, no! Say he will be spared.

GHOST PRESENT: Nope, can't do that, sorry. Unless SOMEONE decides to change... hint, hint.

BOB: A Christmas toast to my boss, Mr. Scrooge! The founder of the feast!

MRS. CRATCHIT: *(angrily)* Oh sure, Mr. Scrooge! If he were here I'd give him a piece of my mind to feast upon. What an odious, stingy, hard, unfeeling man!

BOB: Dear, it's Christmas day. He's not THAT bad. *(Pause)* He's just... THAT sad. *(BOB holds up his bowl)* Come on, kids, to Scrooge! He probably needs it more than us!

MARTHA & TINY TIM: *(holding up their bowls)* To Scrooge!

MRS. CRATCHIT: *(muttering)* Thanks for nothing.

BOB: That's not nice.

MARTHA: And we Cratchits are ALWAYS nice. Read the book, Mom.

MRS. CRATCHIT: Sorry.

(the CRATCHIT FAMILY exits)

SCROOGE: She called me odious! Do I really smell that bad?

GHOST PRESENT: Odious doesn't mean you stink. Although in this case you do... According to the dictionary, odious means "unequivocally detestable." I mean, you are a toad sometimes Mr. Scrooge.

SCROOGE: Wow... that's kind of... mean.

Sneak peek of
Two Gentlemen of Verona for Kids

ANTONIO: It's not nothing.

PROTEUS: Ahhhhh......It's a letter from Valentine, telling me what a great time he's having in Milan, yeah... that's what it says!

ANTONIO: Awesome! Glad to hear it! Because, you leave tomorrow to join Valentine in Milan.

PROTEUS: What!? Dad! No way! I don't want... I mean, I need some time. I've got some things to do.

ANTONIO: Like what?

PROTEUS: You know...things! Important things! And stuff! Lots of stuff!

ANTONIO: No more excuses! Go pack your bag. *(ANTONIO begins to exit)*

PROTEUS: Fie!

ANTONIO: What was that?

PROTEUS: Fiii......ne with me, Pops! *(ANTONIO exits)* I was afraid to show my father Julia's letter, ==lest he should take exceptions to my love==; and my own lie of an excuse made it easier for him to send me away.

ANTONIO: *(Offstage)* Proteus! Get a move on!!

PROTEUS: Fie!!!

(exit)

ACT 2 SCENE 1

(enter VALENTINE and SPEED following)

VALENTINE: Ah, Silvia, Silvia! *(heavy sighs)*

SPEED: *(mocking)* Madam Silvia! Madam Silvia! Gag me.

VALENTINE: Knock it off! You don't know her.

SPEED: Do too. She's the one that you can't stop staring at. Makes me wanna barf.

VALENTINE: I do not stare!

SPEED: You do. AND you keep singing that silly love song. *(sing INSERT SAPPY LOVE SONG)* You used to be so much fun.

VALENTINE: Huh? *(heavy sigh, starts humming SAME LOVE SONG)*

SPEED: Never mind.

VALENTINE: I have loved her ever since I saw her. Here she comes!

SPEED: Great. *(to audience)* Watch him turn into a fool.

(enter SILVIA)

VALENTINE: Hey, Silvia.

SILVIA: Hey, Valentine. What's goin' on?

VALENTINE: Nothin'. What's goin' on with you?

SILVIA: Nothin'.

(pause)

VALENTINE: What are you doing later?

SILVIA: Not sure. Prob-ly nothin'. You?

VALENTINE: Me neither. Nothin'.

SILVIA: Yea?

VALENTINE: Probably.

SPEED: *(to audience)* Kill me now.

SILVIA: Well, I guess I better go.

VALENTINE: Oh, okay! See ya'..

(pause)

SILVIA: See ya' later maybe?

VALENTINE: Oh, yea! Maybe! Yea! Okay!

SILVIA: Bye.

VALENTINE: Bye!

(exit SILVIA)

SPEED: *(aside)* Wow. *(to VALENTINE)* Dude, what the heck was that?

VALENTINE: I think she has a boyfriend. I can tell.

SPEED: Dude! She is so into you! How could you not see that?

VALENTINE: Do you think?

SPEED: Come on. We'll talk it through over dinner. *(to audience)* Fool. Am I right?

(exit)

Sneak peek of
Alice in Wonderland for Kids

(ALICE and CHESHIRE CAT enter; ALICE sees his big grin)

ALICE: *(to audience)* Do you see that? I didn't know cats COULD grin.

CHESHIRE CAT: We can and most of us do. It's because I'm a Cheshire cat.

ALICE: Cheshire cat!? You can grin AND talk!?

CHESHIRE CAT: Among other things.

ALICE: Awesome! Can you tell me which way to go?

CHESHIRE CAT: Where do you want to go?

ALICE: I don't care.

CHESHIRE CAT: Then, it doesn't matter.

ALICE: Well, I want to go SOMEWHERE!

CHESHIRE CAT: You're sure to get somewhere if you walk long enough.

ALICE: Ugh! So, you're a PHILOSOPHICAL, grinning, talking, cat?

CHESHIRE CAT: Listen, the Hatter lives that way and the March Hare lives this way visit either you like, they're both mad.

ALICE: I don't want to be around mad people!

CHESHIRE CAT: We're all mad here. I'm mad. You're mad.

ALICE: I'M not mad!

CHESHIRE CAT: Are you here?

ALICE: Well, yes...

CHESHIRE CAT: Then, you have to be mad!

ALICE: How do you know you're mad?

CHESHIRE CAT: Think of a dog.

ALICE: Okay.

CHESHIRE CAT: When a dog's happy it wags its tail and when it's mad it growls. Well, when I'm angry I wag my tail and when I'm happy I growl. Therefore, I'm mad! See? *(purrs)*

ALICE: No. Anyway, you're purring, not growling.

CHESHIRE CAT: Hmmm, agree to disagree. Are you playing croquet with the Queen?

ALICE: I haven't been invited, yet.

CHESHIRE CAT: I'll see you there! *("vanishes" by putting on black cloak)*

ALICE: Where did you go? *(CHESHIRE "reappears" by removing cloak)* AHHH, don't do that!!

CHESHIRE CAT: Which way will you go?

ALICE: I don't know.

CHESHIRE CAT: Hmmm... Not sure where that is. *("vanishes" again; ALICE walks across stage; CHESHIRE "reappears" behind her)* Did you say know or go?

ALICE: Ah!! Will you stop doing that?!

CHESHIRE CAT: Sorry! *(slowly pulls on the cloak to disappear until only a grin is visible)* Is that better?

ALICE: Barely. *(to audience)* I've often seen a cat without a grin, but a grin without a cat. It's most curious!

CHESHIRE CAT: Bye-bye...

ABOUT THE AUTHORS

KHARA C. BARNHART first fell in love with Shakespeare in 8th grade after reading Hamlet, and she has been an avid fan ever since. She studied Shakespeare's works in Stratford-upon-Avon, and graduated with a degree in English from UCLA. Khara is lucky to have a terrific career and a charmed life on the Central Coast of CA, but what she cherishes most is time spent with her husband and children. She is delighted to have this chance to help kids foster their own appreciation of Shakespeare in a way that is educational, entertaining, and most importantly, fun!

BRENDAN P. KELSO came to writing modified Shakespeare scripts when he was taking time off from work to be at home with his newly born son. "It just grew from there". Within months, he was being asked to offer classes in various locations and acting organizations along the Central Coast of California. Originally employed as an engineer, Brendan never thought about writing. However, his unique personality, humor, and love for engaging the kids with The Bard has led him to leave the engineering world and pursue writing as a new adventure in life! He has always believed, "the best way to learn is to have fun!" Brendan makes his home on the Central Coast of California and loves to spend time with his wife and kids.

Made in the USA
San Bernardino, CA
09 March 2020